P9-BZF-262

5/08
E

# FRANK ASCH

# The Earth and I

Voyager Books • Harcourt, Inc.

Orlando   Austin   New York   San Diego   London

Requests for permission to make copies of any part of the
work should be submitted online at www.harcourt.com/contact or
mailed to the following address: Permissions Department, Harcourt, Inc.,
6277 Sea Harbor Drive, Orlando, Florida 32887-6777.

www.HarcourtBooks.com

First Voyager Books edition 2008

*Voyager Books* is a trademark of Harcourt, Inc., registered in the
United States of America and/or other jurisdictions.

The Library of Congress has cataloged the hardcover edition as follows:
Asch, Frank.
The earth and I/Frank Asch.
p.   cm.
Summary: A child explains how he and the Earth
dance and sing together and take turns listening to each other.
[1. Earth—Fiction.]   I. Title.
PZ7.A778Ear   1994
E—dc20      93-237
ISBN 978-0-15-200443-9
ISBN 978-0-15-206395-5 pb

A C E G H F D B

The paintings in this book were done in watercolors, acrylics,
and colored pencils on Arches watercolor paper, series 500.
The display type was set in Billy.
The text type was set in Columbus.
Color separations by Bright Arts, Ltd., Singapore
Printed and bound by Tien Wah Press, Singapore
Production supervision by Christine Witnik
Designed by Trina Stahl and Lori J. McThomas

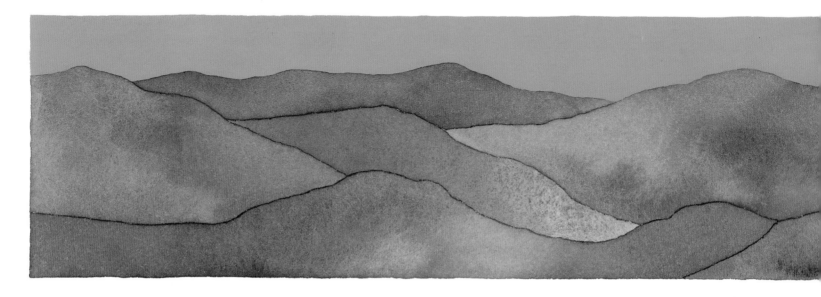

*for Lynne and Eric*

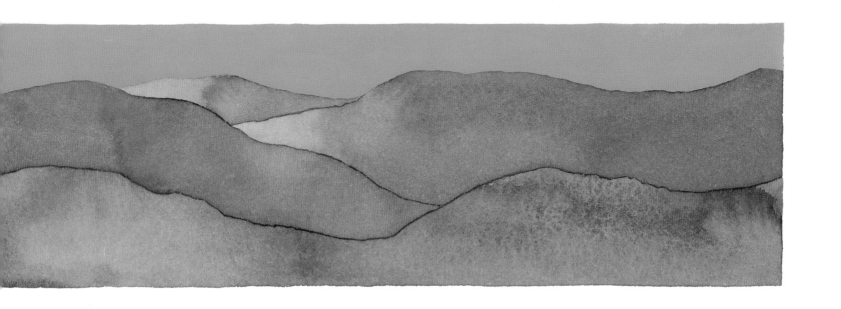

The Earth and I are friends.

Sometimes we go for long walks together.

I tell her what's on my mind.

She listens to every word.

Then I listen to her.

The Earth and I are friends.

We play together in my backyard.

I help her to grow.

She helps me to grow.

I sing for her.

She sings for me.

I dance for her.

She dances for me.

When she's sad,

I'm sad.

When she's happy,

I'm happy.

The Earth and I are friends.